D1223219

Let's Get Active™

LET'S PLAY

FOOTBALL

Shane McFee

PowerKiDS press.
New York

Published in 2008 by The Rosen Publishing Group, Inc.
29 East 21st Street, New York, NY 10010

First Edition

Editors: Nicole Pristash and Jennifer Way
Book Design: Greg Tucker
Photo Researcher: Nicole Pristash

Photo Credits: Cover, pp. 7, 11, 15, 17, 19 by Shutterstock.com; pp. 5, 7 (inset) © www.istockphoto.com; pp. 9, 13 © www.istockphoto.com/Jane Norton; p. 21 © Jeff Hanes/AFP/Getty Images.

Library of Congress Cataloging-in-Publication Data

McFee, Shane.
  Let's play football / Shane McFee. — 1st ed.
      p. cm. — (Let's get active)
  Includes index.
  ISBN 978-1-4042-4192-3 (lib. bdg.)
  1. Football—Juvenile literature. I. Title.
  GV950.7.M34 2008
  796.332—dc22

                                    2007029173

Manufactured in the United States of America

Contents

America's Biggest Sport

Have you ever played football? It is America's most-watched sport. Many different kinds of **athletes** play football. Some football players are very strong. Others are fast runners. The most well-known football players are **professionals**. They play for the National Football League. This is also called the NFL. College and high-school football are also very popular. If college players are good enough, they play for the NFL after they finish school.

This book will tell you about football and some of its most important rules. It will also tell you how you can start playing football yourself.

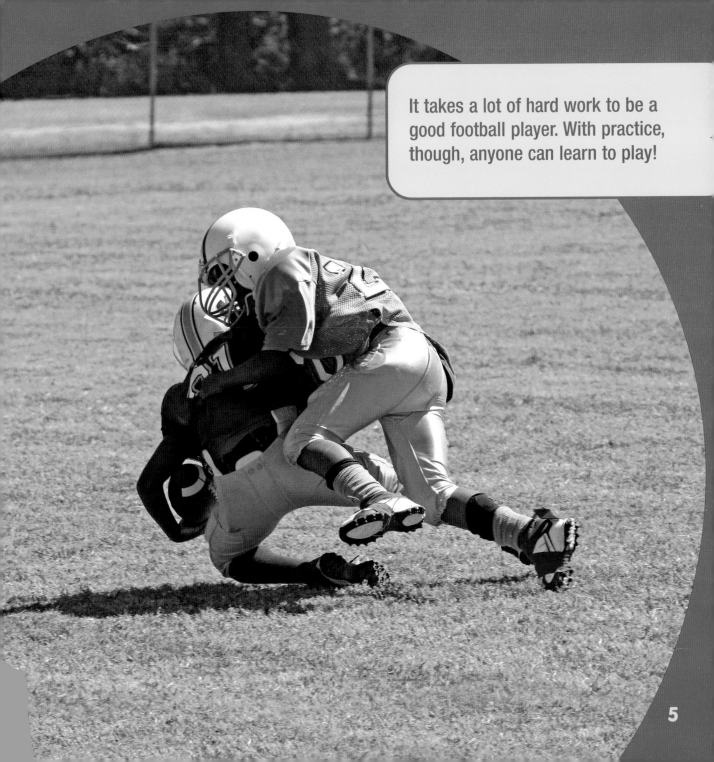

It takes a lot of hard work to be a good football player. With practice, though, anyone can learn to play!

Soccer + Rugby + Time = Football

Football has been around for over 100 years. That might seem like a long time, but football is really still a young sport.

Football is **related** to the game of soccer. In fact, soccer is called football in most other countries. Football is also related to a game called rugby. Rugby has been played in the United Kingdom and Ireland for hundreds of years. Like football, rugby is a contact sport. This means you can touch and even **tackle** players on the other team. Over the years, soccer and rugby **evolved** into the game of football that we play and watch today.

Football and soccer use different-shaped balls. Soccer balls are round. *Inset:* Footballs are oblong, or long and oval.

Ouch!

Since football is a contact sport, it can be dangerous. If you want to play football with your friends, you should play touch football. You do not tackle other players in touch football. You tag, or touch, them.

If you play tackle football, you need a uniform. Football uniforms are meant to keep players safe from **injury**. They have shoulder pads, hip pads, and knee pads. The most important part of the football uniform is the helmet. Football helmets are made of a special kind of plastic. The helmet keeps your head safe.

This football player's uniform is complete. The mouth guard on his helmet keeps his mouth safe when he is tackled.

100 Yards and 11 People

Football is played on a football field. The field is measured by yard lines. One yard is 3 feet (91 cm). A football field is 100 yards (91 m) long. That means that the 50-yard line is the middle of the field. At each end of the field is an area called the end zone. Each end zone has a goalpost.

Each football team has 11 players on the field at a time. These players either play **offense** or **defense**. The players on offense try to move the ball closer to the other team's end zone. The players on defense try to guard their end zone.

This is a professional football stadium in Massachusetts. The NFL team called the New England Patriots plays here.

The Rules of the Game

When a team plays offense, it has four downs, or tries, to move the ball forward 10 yards or to score a touchdown. If the offense moves the ball forward 10 yards, it is called getting the first down and earns the team four additional downs. When there are no downs left, it becomes the other team's turn to play offense.

Touchdowns happen when a player brings the ball into the end zone. Touchdowns are worth six points. After a touchdown, a team can score an extra point or a two-point conversion. An extra point is a kick that goes through the goalposts. For a two-point conversion, the team must get the ball into the end zone again.

Sometimes, a team will try to score by kicking the ball between the goalposts. This is called a field goal. It is worth three points.

Offense and Defense

Each football player has a different position on the team. The offense's leader is the quarterback. The quarterback often passes the ball to a wide receiver. He can also pass the ball to a running back, who takes the ball and runs. There are five offensive linemen, who back up the quarterback. The tight end blocks like the linemen, but he also catches passes.

There are also different positions on the defense. Defensive linemen line up in front of the offense. They try to tackle whoever has the ball. Linebackers tackle just like the linemen, but they also break up short passes. Cornerbacks and safeties try to stop wide receivers from catching the ball.

When a play begins, both teams line up over the ball where it last touched the ground. This place is called the line of scrimmage.

The Coach

The coach leads the football team. He comes up with the **strategy**. Strategy is one of the most important parts of football. Football is sometimes compared to the game of chess.

The coach's strategy is made up of different plays. Plays are **formations** and movements of players. Football teams can have hundreds of plays. Football players need to remember every play.

The coach also leads the team's practice. During practice, players run drills that work on their skills. Quarterbacks practice throwing the ball. Running backs practice running and tackling the defense. The defense practices tackling the offense.

Coaches are very important to a football team. They must lead the whole team. Coaches must also work with players one-on-one, like this coach.

Teamwork

Playing football will help you become strong, fast, and **athletic**. The most important thing about football is learning to work with others as a team. This is called teamwork.

Football also teaches you sportsmanship. Sportsmanship is like honor. An athlete who shows good sportsmanship never cheats. In fact, cheating in football can often lead to a **penalty**. Football penalties affect the whole team, not just a single player. Penalties generally move the ball closer to the cheating player's team's end zone. The whole team is hurt by one player's mistake. Good football players have to value teamwork and sportsmanship.

Football players sometimes group together to talk about their team's strategy or to celebrate a good play. This is called a huddle.

Meet Peyton Manning

Have you ever heard of Peyton Manning? You may have seen him play football on television. Manning is the quarterback for the Indianapolis Colts. Manning learned how to play football at a very young age. He comes from a football-playing family. Manning's father, Archie Manning, was one of the best college football players ever to play. He also played in the NFL. Manning's brother Eli is the quarterback for the New York Giants.

Manning learned about football by watching his father play. Now he is one of the most famous players in the NFL. His team won the Super Bowl in 2007. Many people believe Manning is the best quarterback in the history of football.

During his first nine years in the NFL, Peyton Manning threw for 275 touchdown passes!

Let's Get Active

Does football sound like fun? Do you want to play? All you need is a football and a group of friends. Remember, tackle football can be dangerous. You should only play touch football with your friends.

If you want to play tackle football, you should join a football team. Take a look at American Youth Football or NFL Youth Football. Both groups have teams in many **regions** across the United States.

When you get older, you might have the chance to play football in high school and college. Most schools have football teams that play against other schools. Just remember to wear your helmet!